ROCKY ROAD IS MORE THAN

AN ICECREAM

Poetry

By

Jennifer Brown Banks

ISBN: 978-93-6354-814-5

First Edition: 2025
Rs. 200/-

Cyberwit.net
HIG 45 Kaushambi Kunj, Kalindipuram
Allahabad - 211011 (U.P.) India
http://www.cyberwit.net
Tel: +(91) 9415091004
E-mail: info@cyberwit.net

Printed at Repro India Limited.

ACKNOWLEDGMENTS

All glory and honor to God for the things he has done.

To my mom, for cultivating early in me, a love of literature and a sense of self-worth.

To my poetry group (Poets United) for their ongoing friendship and support.

To my family for acceptance, laughter, and strength.

Contents

LET ME SEE YOUR SCARS

Let me see your scars,
Both the physical
And the invisible,
The ones that sometimes
Compromise your potential
To give your all,

Let me see your scars,
Etched like graffiti
On the heart,
The fears that often re-appear
When commitment rears,
The ones left
From yester-years,

Let me see your scars,
Buried deep
Beneath the surface,
Those that question
If love
Is really worth it,

Let me see your scars,
And I'll show you mine…

HE'S TEACHING MY BODY BRAILLE...

No words
No need…
He knows
My needs,

He reads
Instinctively,
The unspoken

Knows
How to speak this body's language
Fluently
Skillfully
Steadily
Patiently—
Like it was meant to be,
Like heaven sent me,
Every curve,
Every pulsating nerve,
Every thing I deserve,

Eyes closed,
Hearts open,
Muffled sounds
Abound

In the darkness
Of night
He gives such
Sweet delight
His touch
Speaks **VOLUMES**

"ROCKY ROAD" IS MORE THAN AN ICE CREAM...

2023
Becomes the year
To persevere,
To hold God
Closely near

Global shootings
Mass looting
Canadian fires
Polluting,

Supreme court decisions
Render landmark revisions,
Job woes,
Financial lows,

The eternal loss of my long-time lover,
Then a brother,
Friends and others,

A heavy load
So many bumps
On the proverbial road,
Detours
Unexpected turns
Painful lessons

Learned
Stripes earned,

Deferred dreams—
Rocky road
Is more than an ice cream
It seems…

PARENTING IS LIKE BAKING A CAKE

You take the best
Ingredients,
Combine, incorporate
With exacting measures,

Carefully
Follow directives,
Add
A heaping helping
Of love,

Mix,
Mold,
Hover over,

Say a silent prayer,
That your
Painstaking efforts
Will ultimately yield
Something
You can be
Proud of,

And hope
It rises

2004

The year
I discovered
Keanu Reeves,
The joys of unemployment,
FaceBook,
And self-preservation,

When I learned that
Everybody in your family
Ain't necessarily in your corner,

And that a green thumb
Can be cultivated by
A late bloomer,

Was seduced
By the soulful sounds
Of Norah Jones,
The corner café,
And the pleasure
Of my own company,

Said goodbye
To episodes
Of Frazier
And friends,

And Oprah made fifty,

The country was
On the periphery
Of war,

And my boomerang boyfriend
Made a comeback,

I discovered
That God will sometimes
Shake you up
To move you forward,

And poetry
Can sometimes be
A saving grace.

POETS/WE'RE A COOL CROWD

We're a cool crowd,
Dare I say out loud?

More cerebral
Than social,
Part messenger,
Part minstrel,

You and me,
Wired differently,
In good company,

Sharing lineage profoundly
With a royal family
That gave birth proudly
To
Lord Byron
Robert Frost
Langston Hughes
Gwendolyn Brooks
And bards
who hang out regularly
Amid pages
Of college textbooks,

We're a cool crowd,

Dare I say out loud,
Slumping over keyboards
To Show
Poise on paper,

For those
Willing to receive,
Our hearts worn
On sleeves,
Like
Fashion accessories

A Checkered Past

His past,
Was "checkered",
Like
A winter quilt,
Like flannel pajamas,
Like a tablecloth in
An Italian eatery—

Woven into
Each pattern and intersecting line,
Through adversity and time,
He was being divinely refined

And through his trials and tribulations,
And his evolution,
Through the process,
He found God,

And God led him to me
When both
Were ready

AT THE CROSSROADS

Red light
Green light,

Should I stop
Should I go?

My heart says yes,
My mind says no,

Red light
Green light,
Hold on tight

As we journey
The path of discovery
To explore
Love's possibilities

CORNBREAD

Rich
In calories
Richer
In memories
Of momma
And me,
Her legacy
Of feeding folks' needs,

Cooking?
For her
A ministry,
Cornbread,
A specialty,
Sans recipe,
She prepares instinctively,
A pinch hcrc,
A dash there,
With love and care,

These thoughts,
Thoughts of yesteryear,
As I fight back
Today's tears
Wishing she
Were still here,

This cold winter morning,
While cornbread fixing…
She's the one ingredient missing

OPEN WIDE

Sometimes
Life's lessons
Can be like Medicine—
It's important to ingest them
To process them
To take as prescribed—

The better you'll feel,
The sooner you'll heal

On the other side of today's pain
Awaits tomorrow's gain,

So open wide
Master the lesson,
Take your medicine...

EXPECT 2 B SURPRISED

Expect 2 B surprised
By the kindness
Of strangers
And the betrayal
Of so-called friends,

By how true love
Can transform your
False beliefs,

By the value of good choices
And how many decisions
In life
Are simply
Out of your control,

By how strong you can really be
When you've been dealt
A losing hand,
By God's blessings…

Expect the unexpected

IN 'DA HOOD

Scores of
Liquor stores
And beauty parlors
Erected by investors,
Cuz they buy
Into the lie
That folks of color
Only want to look "fly"
And get high,

Bars bolted
On windows
Folks
Caged in like animals
To protect from evil
From potential criminals,

Where at night
Sirens lull you to sleep,
Cuz peace don't keep,
Neighbors don't speak,
Poverty…
Knee deep,

Food deserts
That stretch for

Country miles
Help to feed
Unhealthy lifestyles
And premature demise,

A place where
Generic mentalities
Shape a false reality
That life
Holds no more
Than what is seen
Outside these doors

PARADOX

Part intellect
Part rough-neck
As I reflect...

Love the way he
Serves
And protects

The way
We connect
In ways
I didn't expect

EMOTIONAL MAYDAY

Needing
Wanting
Weary
Restless
Wanting
Rescue
Will you?

REPEAT.

ON THE OTHER SIDE OF THIS...

On the other side/of this pandemic
There's a message that persists
Perhaps
A divine lesson that exists
Beyond logistics?

Is it a wake up call
For us all?
A curse
For living outside
Of God's laws?

A reminder
To live kinder?
A warning to repent?
Prelude
Of an apocalyptic event?

The dawning of a new day?

No one can clearly say...

But what I believe
For sure,
If we are to endure

And overcome this,
God must be the “cure”

For this situation
Is truly demanding,
And exceeds our human capacity
For understanding,

So at the end of the day
Let us bow our knees
And humbly pray
This virus away

504 HOURS

3 weeks ago today
Since he was last here
504 hours
Since his smooth talk
Landed his smooth skin
Next to mine

And I can
Still smell,
(Mentally inhale)
Hints of his
Grey Flannel cologne
Against my pink
Cotton sheets

Still remember
How his touch made me forget,
Still remember
The rain cascading
Outside my bedroom window,
As I watched him sleep—
Plop, plop
Plop, plop
Still remember

DON'T WATER DEAD PLANTS

Don't water dead plants
Their season
Has come and gone
As are the wasted tears
That fall in vain
Over the love
I once felt for you,
The love I once knew

Now withered
Unable to be resurrected
From lack
Of daily sun
And being rooted in
Infertile soil

...Don't water dead plants

A LOVE LETTER TO GOD

How do I love thee?
Let me count the days,
The ways—
I love thee
From the depths of my soul
From a heart
That's full
And grateful,

Grateful for creature comforts
And blessings galore,

For gifts you've granted
I never asked for—

I love you for the beauty of nature
And children's laughter,
For simple pleasures,
Relationships I treasure,
For quiet times
We spend together—

I love how I feel your divine kiss
Whenever I listen to music
And experience its bliss,

I love you for wiping my tears
For calming my fears,
I love you Lord
For always
Lingering near—

How do I love thee?
Let me count the days,
The ways—
I love you
For loving me
In my imperfection,
For your constant guidance
And protection

Without question,
I love you Lord

TO WRITE POETRY
(A HAIKU)

To write poetry
Is to inscribe on the walls
Of eternity

AINT IT SILLY, REALLY

Ain't it silly, really?

How families part,
As readily as the Red Sea,
Simply because they disagree,
Over ancient history,
Or money,
Or sibling rivalry,
Or hurtful words
Uttered mistakenly,
Ain't it silly, really?

How we undermine
Bloodlines that God assigns
Selfishly

How narratives sometimes differ
Of the same story,
Ultimately
Causing another nut
To fall off the family tree

Ain't it silly, really?

AGEING GRACEFULLY

At night
I used to moan and groan
And carry on
In the throes of ecstasy,

These days,
When I make loud sounds
And tumble around
It's likely
From arthritis
In my left knee,

And might I add
I'm inclined not to find
Lost things as easily
As once before,
I blame their absentia
On growing dementia
(Did I mention I abhor?)

I've swapped sexy stilettos,
(That once gave jiggle to my wiggle)
For orthopedic styles,

A little less attractive,
But they help me stay active
And cause my feet to smile,

The only thing I can "exercise"
If I am wise,
Is self-discipline,

So when possible
I'm tucked in bed by ten p.m.,
And keep my vices to a minimum,

(Let the church say amen!)

These days
As I age,
I'm enjoying simple pleasures,
Embracing friendships
I treasure,

Looking youthful,
Learning
At every measure,

Living more gratefully,
Ageing,
Ever
Gracefully

10 COMMANDMENTS* MY MOTHER'S VERSION

1. Honor thy mother. "I brought you in this world; I can take you out!"
2. The way to a man's heart is through his stomach. Learn to cook and clean well.
3. Always have your own money. Even if it's HIS.
4. Never make Gumbo without fresh ingredients.
5. Always exercise your right to vote. Our ancestors died for the privilege.
6. Get a good education. It does more for your image than designer clothes or well-maintained hair.
7. Take care of your feet and your teeth. It will enhance your golden years.
8. Watch your weight, if you want men to watch you.
9. You get what you pay for.
10. Mom is always right.

M.I.A. ON SUNDAY

I don't need a
Dwelling place
A designated space
A "sacred"
Physical building
To express the depths
Of my feelings,
To honor He
Who "dwells" in me

This body
Is a temple
Where we meet daily,
Intimately
Mind, heart and soul
His virtues I extol

He often speaks to me
Through nature's beauty, imagery and divinity,
Through the pleasure I derive
From my favorite song's melody,
His goodness
I can "taste and see"

Even when you don't find me
Periodically
At church
Please don't find it odd
No matter my G.P.S. location or destination
I AM always in the presence of my God

OH, HENRY!

Sweet,
Like
A to-be-enjoyed treat,
Layered,

Pleasing and fulfilling
Indeed,
It's no wonder
Why a popular
Candy bar
Was named in your honor…
Oh, Henry!

JACKIE'S JOY

(For my sister)

Despite the many blows of life
Despite all the troubles, struggles, and strife
She smiles all the while
With the joy of a child

Because she believes
In the Lord—
Because she believes
That the Lord Restores,

A faithful servant is she,
She lives her life with simplicity

She treasures
Everyday pleasures
Like worshipping with her
Church community,
My home-made peach cobbler,
Dusties music from the fifties,
And collecting old photos of the family,

She enjoys creating new memories,
And being a proud grandma,

She's authentic,
Being a good Christian
Is her earthly mission
Despite worldly conditions—

As the "Good Book" references in scripture,
She has learned to be content
In whatever state she is in

ETERNAL-LEE

You and I share history
(a decade, more specifically)
Something no one can ever
Take from me

But death robbed us
Unexpectedly
Regretfully,

Rest assured
As long as life endures,
A part of me will always love you
Always…
Eternal, Lee

IN THE COURT OF PUBLIC OPINION

In the court of public opinion
Sometimes I've been convicted,
Judged unfairly,
By those who assumed to know me,
By mistaken identity,
By circumstantial evidence
That made no sense

In the court of public opinion
People sometimes
misunderstand your intentions,
Misjudge you,
Some will even Unlove you,
Refuse to give you
The benefit of the doubt,

Just the same
You must
Stay sane
Refrain
From losing your dignity,
Dismiss the negativity,
Stay smart,
Realize that the ultimate "Judge" is God…
And he knows your heart

SAY YES TO HAPPINESS!

Say yes,
Say yes
To happiness!

Make it a welcome guest,
Invite it in
to
Get undressed

Bid farewell
To needless stress

Count the ways
That you've been blessed,

Say yes
To happiness
And no
To the
Endless requests,

To all the dramas
And foolishness,

If need be
Take baby steps,

Say yes
To happiness!

MS. JOYCE

Gentle
Her voice,
Gentle
By choice,
Well-traveled
And poised,

The years
Have served her well,
She'll gladly share her wisdom
If you sit with her
A spell,
Her wise counsel
Born of heart
And soul,
Valuable, like gold
90 years old—
A teacher
Beyond the classroom,
A cherished mother
An animal lover,
Gifted pianist,

She feeds unspoken needs
Through loving deeds,
Through planting seeds
For tomorrow's harvest

A rich and fruitful legacy
Matriarch of her family

DEATH IN LETHAL DOSAGES

We're fed, first spoonfuls, then with gradual increase
The countless lives, the ever-growing demise of the deceased
Nightly news spewed in the form of crime stats
Or those dead,
Due to the Covid-19 spread
The loss of loved ones and friends
Over and over again
Alerted through Facebook updates
And dreaded phone calls
Even celebrity downfalls—

Slowly, surely, causing a reckoning with reality
0ur own mortality
Causing a certain pathology
A sickness of heart
For the exits that never end
The toll it takes on our soul
Wondering when our number will be next
And in effect, causing us to digest life
A little faster
Before we too
Must meet the Master

MANDATE FOR THE MODERN WOMAN

Dear superwoman,
Take rest,
De-stress,
Relinquish the need
To be perfect
Take baby steps—
You got this!

Clear your mind
Of the debris
You find
From negative
Thoughts,
Past regrets,
Foolish gossip—

Take joyful moments
To kick back and relax,
Indulge in things you like to do,
Renew,
Take care of you—
Practice self love,
Without always
Being judged—

Stand tall

Recognize
You don't have to
"Conquer all",
Rome wasn't built over night—

Love your body,
Celebrate the skin you're in,
Make good health
A welcome friend—

Redefine success
Take baby steps,
Resist the need
To always "fix"—
You got this!

LOVE THY NEIGHBOR?

Neither friend
Nor enemy—
Bound by our shared lines/ of owned property,
This
Our only commonality—

Some days
We share forced pleasantries,

Some days
They challenge me,
Infringe on
My sanity,
Disregard
Respectful boundaries,

Some days
Good ones
Seem to be
An anomaly,

Some days
They cause difficulty
To honor biblically
The mandate
To love thy neighbor,

(Particularly the ones not my particular flavor)

Heaven help me!

FLOWERS NOW?

When we die
People cry
Often reminisce
Of times
Gone by,
How we'll be missed—

Share accolades
Of the difference
We've made,
The role we've played,
The joy
We gave—

We're showered
With flowers
(Mostly Lilies)
All lovely, really—

The true tragedy
Is closed eyes
Can't see their beauty,

Closed eyes
That shed tears
For all the yesteryears
That there were
No flowers
When we
Were here

IT'S A DOG'S WORLD

Judge Judy
Rules on the same type of case
On TV today,
For the umpteenth time—
(an animal inflicted wound)

And it appears
The verdict is very clear:

Too many people treat
Their dogs
Like people

And treat people
Like dogs

CHICAGO, THE SUPERHERO

Chicago
Survives,
Thrives,
Defies,
Sleeps
With one eye open,
At all times,

Like a Phoenix,
She rises
Amid ashes,

In spite
Of the great fire,
That threatened to end her,
In spite of
Rampant violence,
Corrupt politicians,
Weather
With its own mind,
Overcrowding,
Disrespect, disregard
Leadership lacking,
Trash talk
From the media,
Trashy neighborhoods,

Budget deficits,
Surplus of sins,
Input
From outsiders,
And mail service
That often
Fails to deliver,

Chicago
Survives,
Thrives,
Defies,
Always
Renewing,
Rebuilding,
Resilient,
Resisting defeat—
Like a superhero
Chicago ain't no punk

TO THE BEST FRIEND I NEVER MET (4 KAREN IN KENTUCKY)

By Divine design
We met online,
And who would ever suspect
We would really "connect"
(in more ways than one)
By way of the Internet,

Two people who couldn't be
More different
Separated by miles
Of distance,
And yet
Couldn't be much closer,

A White lady
Tucked away in the country,
In Kentucky
And a Black chick
From Chicago's big city,

United by literary interests,
And mutual respect,
Communicating through emails, phone calls, and texts
And as I reflect,
You are the best friend
I've never met,

Through the years
We have shared laughter
And tears
Dreams and fears,
Swapped recipes to serve
Those we love dear,

Amid many of life's
Trials and tribulations
You've often been there
To listen and care,

No Hallmark card
Could capture
The bond we share,

A sisterhood of hearts
That's truly rare…

You are a special gift

2020 REMEMBERED

2020
A year remembered
For greater life clarity,
Ushering in
20/20 vision
Most definitely,
A year
For re-establishing
Priorities,
An end
To normalcy,

A year that witnessed
A mysterious virus
World gained,
A mass exodus,
The ushering in
Of pain,

Chaos,
Confusion,
Conversations with God,

A year of isolation,
Endless hours of
Contemplation,

A time
Of separation,

A year
I can't wait
To forget…

HEAD GAMES

Without realizing it,
Sometimes
We let people
Play head games with us,

To do a number on our ego,
Make us feel less,
To make us second guess
Who we are,
What we stand for,
Even our purpose—

Sometimes these "gamers"
Come in the form of a faux friend
A family member
Or your garden variety "hater",
Or a man
Who has yet to know
What it is to truly be a man,

Psyched out,
We fail to see
That this mental manipulation
Often stems
From jealousy,
Or someone's sense of inadequacy,

We fail to realize
That no one's opinion
Should be more important
Than our own,
And that
Self love and acceptance
Is the best strategy
For victory

COOKING IN THE KITCHEN

Momma always taught me
That the way to a man's heart
Was through his stomach,

So I learned
How to burn,
How to earn,
Sometimes
In high heels
With all the frills—

Did my apprenticeship
With Momma,
Martha Stewart,
Julia Child,
Recipes
From relatives,
Cookbooks
From every corner
Of the world,
And some trial and error,
For good measure,
Along the way
Folks would say
My pot roast is legendary,
My peach cobbler is worship worthy,

My skills,
Undeniable—
Momma always taught me
That the way to a man's heart
Was through his stomach,

But what she forgot to tell me,
In feeding his burning desires,
Is if he is ravenous,
He may eat
From more
Than one kitchen

DEAREST BROTHER (4 WARREN)

Spring has begun to sing—
I hear its melody in the trees,
And I feel your presence,
Even amid your earthly absence

As the season surfaces,
I remember how
You
Planted, prepared, pruned
Rose bushes faithfully
That bloom
Year after year,
In my yards
(Usually around mid-may)
Some red, some pink,

And as they blush
In their beauty,

I remember that
Love never dies.

I remember
How much I miss you.

Even now.

www.ingramcontent.com/pod-product-compliance
Ingram Content Group UK Ltd.
Pitfield, Milton Keynes, MK11 3LW, UK
UKHW041316190726
13845UKWH00025B/316

9 789363 548145